PEBBLES TO POEMS

A selection from the published works
2018-2020

Frank Prem

Publication Details

Published by Wild Arancini Press

Title: Pebbles to Poems

ISBN: 978-1-925963-20-5
ISBN: 978-1-925963-17-5 (e-bk)

For the readers.

Without you,
nothing.

Contents

About *Pebbles to Poems*

A publishing adventure

Pebbles to Poems is a collection of extracts from six collections of poetry published in print and digital formats between November 2018 and July 2020.

The first three collections – *Small Town Kid, Devil In The Wind*, and *The New Asylum* – are either broadly autobiographical or true-life experiential. Together, they comprise a series of memoirs.

These collections reflect growing up in rural and semi-isolated Australia during the 1960s and 70s, living through the terrible wildfires of 2009, known in Australia as Black Saturday, and a personal experience of psychiatry, from growing up in a mental asylum town as a child, to student nursing in the institution and on to a career as a psychiatric nurse in the public mental health system

These three poetry collections comprise a unique experience of poetry as the vehicle for conveying lived experiences, telling all a reader needs to know, while allowing the imagination to carry the reading away into the readers own experiences and imagination.

The second half of *Pebbles to Poems* revisits A Love Poetry Trilogy, comprised of three stand-alone collections – *Walk Away Silver Heart, A Kiss for the Worthy,* and *Rescue and Redemption.*

A Love Poetry Trilogy was drew on three poems from a century or more ago, written by wonderful poets (Amy Lowell – Madonna of the Evening Flowers, Walt Whitman – Leaves of Grass, and T.S. Eliot – The Love Song of J. Alfred Prufrock) and to utilize each line or phrase as the basis or inspiration for a new piece of work.

A joyous project that resulted in three very different explorations of love – love for another, love of the world and an individuals place within it, and a search for love through unexpected places.

I hope you enjoy these poems, and urge you to go on and buy a copy of the originals for your own bookshelves and bedside tables. Links to each collection are provided, throughout.

FP

Small Town Kid

Title: **Small Town Kid**
ISBN: 978-0-9751442-3-7 (pbk)
ISBN: 978-0-9751442-4-4 (e-bk)

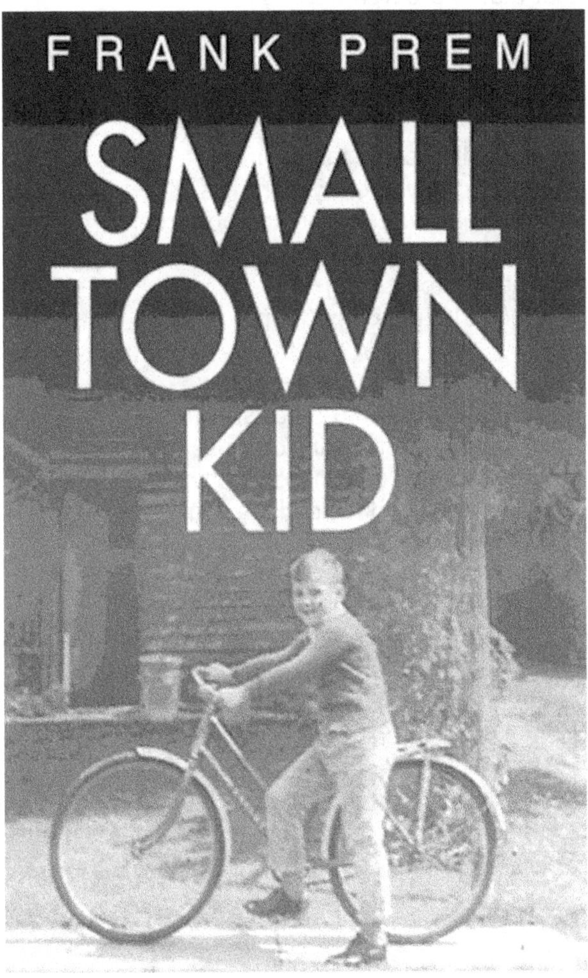

I can hardly wait to show you

july is finally gone and I am breathing
in the air of august
a taste of weather
that teases promise of days
when the sun is warm again
and the shivers worn since may
can be packed away for another season

I can hardly wait to take you
to the places where my spirit lies
along singing waters and scrubby creeks
the green and granite-bouldered hills
that never stop calling
and won't let me deny them

I want to show you where I grew
and what I saw when I was small
if something still remains of those things
so clearly drawn as pictures in my mind
of a small boy and his curious dog
with a long way to travel from breakfast
to the distant darkness of evening
on so many shining days

will you walk with me on a balmy afternoon
in the mayday hills and the woolshed valley
along the silver creek and past apple orchards
to the places where rabbits went to ground
at the sound of approaching adventurers
crossing old scars left by miners seeking gold dust
where I also found small treasures once

take my hand in the main street
of this town hewn from honey granite
I will tell you what once stood here and there
and you might help me rediscover what I knew

when I was in the springtime of my life
before an autumn season comes
to settle on my shoulders

I can hardly wait to show you

oma rocks the cradle

while mama works
oma rocks the cradle
lulling the child
into slumber

the rhythm
soothes and settles

peace in the house

the afternoon passes
calm

~

in the early hours
fretful waking

dragging darkness

broken sleep

a weary journeying
to work
in the thinness
of morning

why will the child
not sleep
every blessed night
what is wrong with him

~

while mama works
oma
rocks the cradle

working for a generation

a small boy is at play

an older man
sits close by
on a chair
in contemplation
of what has been done
what progress made

considering the challenge
for tomorrow

a tree has been felled
and a photograph taken
to prove the victory

when the clean-up
is done
a garden will be dug
fruit trees planted

the man and his grown son
have laboured
and the days to come
will be the same
but
when finished
this work will stand
through generations

the boy is crying
calling to be picked up
and held

an encouraging word
and the lad rises

wandering closer
still sobbing
lying down again
this time at the old man's feet

his *opa* picks him up
and holds him
sitting in the chair
at the end
of the day
until the tears have stopped

frenki boy

mama called me
frenki boy
when I was a child
sometimes she said it
frenki yoy!
to make a point
about trouble I'd be in
if I didn't stop
what I was doing

yoy meni yoy frenki!
I used to get a lot of that
though
for the life of me
I couldn't tell what *yoy*
I might have committed

it was a legacy
maybe
left to a small boy
from this other troubled guy
I used to hear about a bit

he was called
isus boga!
or something like that
and the women would make
a sign of the cross
with their hands
when they said it

but
in the evening
sometimes
mama would kiss me
and I'd become just
frenki moy

times like that
the day would end
okay

you know mum's cooking

you know how sometimes your mum
can be really over the top
with cooking traditional food in the way
that she learned to do it back home
and most of the time it's sort of okay
or you don't really notice because
it's just there all the time
and sometimes it's really good
and you can feel clever about it
because the other kids' mums
don't know how to cook that good stuff
but sometimes it's that rotten spicy mince
wrapped up in cabbage leaves or
stuffed into capsicum and drowned
in some kind of red stewy sauce

you know *sarma* and *sattarash*

well I hate 'em

loss of faith

it is the women of my family
who are the keepers of faith
every sunday
and sometimes in the week
either early or late
in dresses that are restrained but fine
and with shawls rather than hats
to cover the head

our women wear no hats
but they pray
for the men and for the children
the passing over of our sins
and for those they left behind
in search of a better life
for their young

it is the women
who round up the men and the boys
to ensure attendance
at the small cathedral in the town
on the important days
for ritual expressions of faith

but when the letter for my mother came
in black-lined airmail
from the village of her parents
she wept with the bitterness
of injustice and loss and grief
she cried for so long
I was afraid
she would never stop

god lost a believer
and I no longer needed
to make an appearance
at the sunday mass

Devil In The Wind

Title: **Devil In The Wind**
ISBN: 978-0-9751442-6-8 (pbk)
ISBN: 978-0-9751442-7-5 (e-bk)

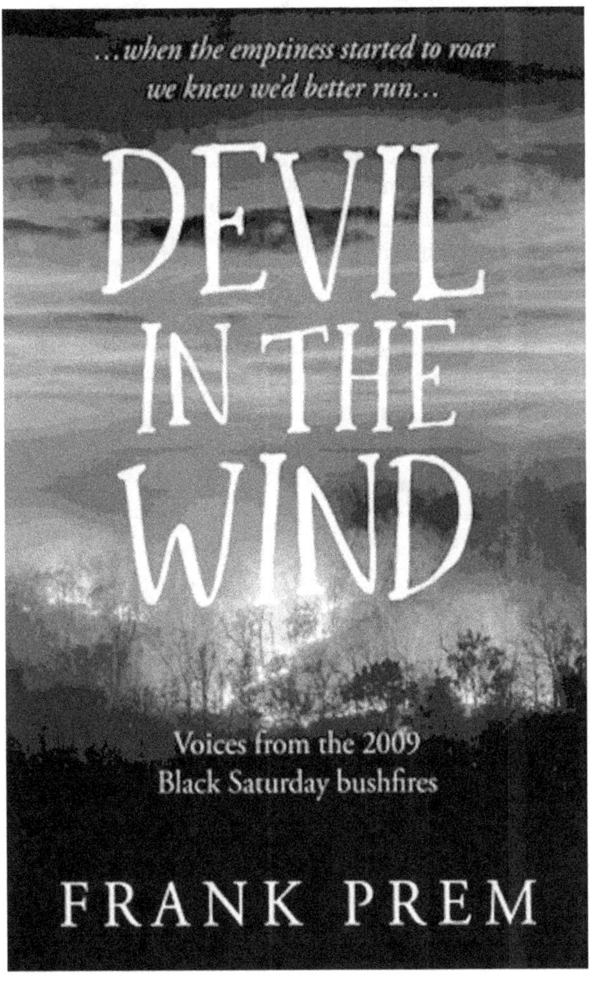

callignee butterflies

butterflies have always lived
in our meadow

you can see them moving
everywhere you turn
in little flits
out of the corner of your eye

on this land we cleared
to make our home
they're as much a part
of every small thing
as we are

on black saturday
we might have gone
or might have stayed

there was nothing
to give us advice
better than our eyes
fixed on the thick smoke
at the back of the hill

when the air turned still
around us
it could have meant anything

in that eerie silence
who would know

but ten tiny wraiths
fluttered to the floor
of our lounge room
looking for safety
as low down as they could get

and when the emptiness
started to roar we knew
we'd better run

it was time to go

evidence to the commission of inquiry: overview

1

well
the people up in the hills
where we live
were all chasing an uncomplicated ideal

for instance
my wife never watched tv
or opened up the daily paper

you see
all of us wanted to get away from that
and the whole town was full of people
who were much the same

yes it was hot that day
and yes
the blistering wind came from the north
but we're used to that
so the first I knew anything
of firestorms
was a blossom rising red
in the paddock stubble
of the block next door

I went out
to hurry up the neighbours
told them
now was time for them to go

and I waited at the bottom of the hill
for my wife and my son
until the leaf litter beneath my feet
began to glow

then I had to turn away

2

we didn't hear any warnings
over the radio
or anything like that
but
it was raining gum leaves
from out of the trees
for days and nights beforehand
so we knew something was up

3

I said to my wife

that fire's out of control

4

the guys in charge of the firefighters
thought marysville was still okay
but the place had already become ash and corpses
the night before

5

from the operations room
it was hard to keep track
and to know where was most needy

who to focus on

there were hundreds of fires on the go
by that stage

6

the sound I heard
was like ten or twelve jumbo jets
down at the airport

all screaming their guts out
at the same time

7

well
before lunchtime on that day
I'd have said the fire-response system
in this state
was second to none
in the entire world

yes
that's what I would have told you
then

fire plan lament

I've heard
that my lifetime
has been an era of change

almost nothing
is the same
now
as it was when I was born

cars and planes
takeaway food
a computer and a phone
in every pocket

I couldn't have imagined
when I was small
that living an alternate life
online
could replace the summer days
that I spent walking in the bush
with my dog

but I suppose
you only really notice such things
when you look behind

we used to put the fires out
by hand
with wetted hessian bags
and knapsacks

and somehow
we always seemed
to beat them down
or douse them

bulldozers
would carve a nine-foot break
to make the fires stop
it was rare for a blaze
to ever leap the line

greenies weren't impressed
of course
said they made an ugly gash
in the forest

too wide
and to the detriment of nature

nowadays you can't go in
without proper training
too many *fire-ies* have been crisped
beside their machines

occupational health and safety
means most of the time
you just have to stand back
and let the red bastard run

a firebreak today
means trying to surround it
pushing the whole forest in
for acres all around
so eventually it'll eat itself out
cannibalised and starved

but it does no good
not really
because the bush is drier now
and these fires burn so hot

the wind
will nurture a shower of sparks
for miles at a time
and it doesn't rain any more
when you need it to

once upon a time you knew
the a change in the weather
would come
carrying good rain
to cool it all down

but today I'm listening to sky cranes
dumping water
just the other side
of a brown billowing plume

and they're saying it again
on the radio
get your fire plans ready

shit
all they really mean is
make up your minds
will you stay or will you go

and god bless you if you stay
when you've seen what happened
to those other poor tryers last week
didn't matter what they chose
they died just as dead whether at home
or out on the road

I'm tired of it
I wasn't born to meet change
the way it's happening now

I don't learn very well
under the pressure of my arse
being half incinerated

if this is how it has to be
then there's nothing *new*
that I really know

but I learnt at the breast
that you stay with it
right through to the very end

so this is my fire plan:
stand and fight
take the worst that comes

if I'm still upright when it's over
I'll shout the beer

If not
I'll see you on the other side
and it'll be your turn
to buy

evidence to the commission of inquiry: the warning

I work as a spotter in the towers
over the summer months

my place is up on the ridge
about three k's out of marysville

from there on a clear day
I can see away off
to the horizon

when the first plume rises
it's my job to note coordinates
then get onto the airwaves
so the brigades can get there
to put it down

on that saturday I saw the first smoke
over by murrindindi mill
then it was over the top
around the black range
travelling west

I was on the line
as fast as I could make the call
because I could see
this thing would be big

but the radio did nothing
and the mobile phone wasn't answered
by the third failed call I knew
some people were going to die

marysville is down in a hollow
and I didn't think it stood a chance
the smoke hit a thousand feet
and all the reply I got was
busy

I rang a friend
and told her to get out
because the fire bearing down
was a beastly size

I saw a spotfire light up
fourteen kilometres ahead of the front
while I was on the phone

I saw it begin to run
and then
I felt terrified

the clouds went up another thousand feet
and ash and embers started falling
in a sort of hot black rain

the thing was alive
and I just shouted
good luck
down the phone
then
I bolted

they're saying that marysville
had no warning
but it's as true as I'm standing here
it wasn't because I didn't try

chardy at the cellar door

henry and ev
put a shipping container underground
to make a wine cellar

when the smoke turned into flame
there was nowhere else to go

henry's still shaking his head
about the door
glowing red
while they watched

held prisoner
by the heat and the smell

he said

what else could we do
we were feeling
quite shell-shocked
and knew we might die

as the hours passed we drank
five bottles

screw-top chardonnay I think it was
and a little too warm at that

but I couldn't crack the grange
without a bottle opener

evidence to the commission of inquiry: next time

we prepared meticulously for months
ahead of the hot season
cleared away any fuel and cut the grass

made sure there were no trees
too close to the house

we were ready

when the fire rating came across
on the warning system
I knew it was going to be bad
but figured the numbers had to be wrong
because years back to ash wednesday
which was a shocking set of fires
the rating only reached into the sixties
and on this day
it was hitting a hundred and sixty-five

still
we were ready
but my wife was so worried about it
that she rang everyone around us
all the young families
to tell them they should go

I think a few lives were saved
because of what she did

we first saw a bit of smoke
off in the distance
and then black embers started to drop

my wife went to put out a spotfire
but the soles on her shoes melted
when she jumped on the flames

we retreated to the house
and then the power failed

I shot out to the shed
to start the pump
but the petrol was all gone

evaporated

the wind changed and I got burned

as we ran
the house went up
just behind us

yes
we thought we were pretty right
to fight the fire that day
but every time I look
at the bandages on my arms
and the distorted face I see in the mirror
I tell myself
we need to do it better
next time

The New Asylum

Title: **The New Asylum**
ISBN: 978-0-9751442-8-2 (pbk)
ISBN: 978-0-9751442-5-1 (e-bk)

mental health creature

some things
live within the blood

from when I was a child
riding my bicycle
to visit *up top*
where my parents toiled
in the old lunatic asylum
discreetly perched
behind the ha-ha wall
I was shaped
to the tasks and functions
of working in mental health

movement into other fields
and naïve dreams
of becoming something
with more glamorous potential
were inevitably fleeting

in the end
after long years
I have come back
and am again that creature
a psychiatric nurse
toiling
in the eternal asylums
of mental health

a ha-ha above town

there is always a hill
in a mental-asylum town

the ha-ha wall
and the poor fools it protects
and embraces within fine examples
of long-outdated architecture
perches half-concealed
from the gaze
of the good citizens
resident down below

for unlike the near-normal presence
of convicted criminals
in the prison close to the centre
of the township
insanity is unsightly
frightening in the nakedness it reveals
and there is just a possibility
of contagion

atop the hill and behind the wall
out of averted sight
the asylum lies camouflaged
by green acres of gardens
carefully tended
and flourishing farmland
for the production
of vegetables
milk and meat

hidden away despite the prosperity
that a thousand lost souls
living within have ensured
for the past present and future
of the townsfolk
who depend on this location of insanity
to earn

or otherwise access
their daily bread and butter

and it is here
that a young boy's mother
will be shown how to be a ward assistant
and here that his father
will become a kitchenhand in the messroom
and both will learn to be victorian public servants

it is here that the daily journey
to the inside of the ha-ha
above the town
begins

taxi shuttle

every morning
at ten minutes to seven
blue uniforms
starched and stiff
cluster in the spilling light
at the front
of the post office

breath misting
in the pre-dawn cold
of a winter's day

four at a time
in the taxi shuttle
up the hill
for the start
of another shift
in the back wards

opening the door; surveying the realm

this is not a locked ward
it is classified
open: acute
I checked

but I am standing
waiting
for staff to open up
and let me enter

to notice that I am here

there is a gaggle of them
talking in the nurses' station

they are too busy
to pay attention

~

and this is it
my new ward
the ward of rumour
and innuendo

the place of raised eyebrows
and a muttered
good luck
when it is mentioned
when my new role
is spoken of

this is that place

so many lost souls
directionless
falling under the sway

and barely existing
within these crazy walls
day after day

it seems tragic

and then
there are the patients

not a lot anymore

we're standing in the staff courtyard
it's break time
and we're doing coffee and a cigarette
when he says to me

I've always worked in psych
I love it

I've never been tempted
by anything else

it's changed though
from the old days
oh
a hell of a lot really

he takes a deep drag
lets out the blue smoke
of a reflective moment
has another sip from the styrofoam cup
and says

you know what

about a year ago
we had a real old-fashioned case come in
like we used to get
in the old days

no drugs
no family history
no obvious causes
just crazy

mad as a cut snake actually

it was a first presentation
and it took a while
but we fixed him up
he got better and we turned him loose
he hasn't been back

that's what I like best
good straightforward madness
that you can do something with

but you don't see much of that
anymore

final discharge

in its serenity
the town cemetery is a beautiful place
the granite work and the statuary
hold a sombre dignity
in the peaceful air

a contrast
to unmarked mounds that are
little more than gentle blemishes
in the waving grass
that surrounds a wandering path

many histories lie here
pioneer spirit and gold
plague disease and chinese ceremonial
anglican
jewish
catholic
and unwanted

on the left side
towards the back
inconspicuous and out of the way
are those unclaimed who are
at last
in possession of their final discharge

released
from the paternal care
of the mental asylum

consumers now

in the game
they're referred to
as consumers now
with service delivered
to a place called home

but I used to know them
a little better than that

they were
ella and ferdie and max
and eddie and pinky and b-ee-ill

they're long gone
and never come to mind
except on visits
to deserted dayrooms
and haunted dormitories

Walk Away Silver Heart

Title: **Walk Away Silver Heart**
ISBN: 978-1-925963-06-9 (pbk)
ISBN: 978-1-925963-01-4 (e-bk)

a small piece (free)

All day long I have been working

all the day
I
am working

toil
required to keep fuel
on the fire

and the table
well laden

I do
what I must
to ensure
all is
what it should be

yet
through each of those hours
I dream

inhabit
desire

and a yearning

to be home
to be with you

to be one
with my own spaces and places
well known

defined

all the day long
I have been
working as I know I must do
but
all the day long
too
I have nurtured
my heart

kept a piece
one small piece of it
free
and untrammelled
by need

or other
mundane requirement

I have placed it
in my mind
right there
beside you

our backs
warmed together
by fire

well nourished (now to sleep)

Now I am tired

I have gazed
up
at the sky
all morning

placed my nose
right in close
to smell
the sweet perfume
that comes
from blossom

in the garden
I have studied
the ways that green grass
grows

noting
that it did not move
at all
like this
in the winter

and listening
to birds
has taken more time
than anticipated

until
I find the day has fled
on wings
while I pursued it
on foot

I am tired now
with
nothing done

I am wearied
from my thoughts
and observations

I do believe
I need to rest
or
my senses may
explode

but this day

this wondrous day
has brought nourishment
for my soul

from a confusion (of insensible things)

I call: "Where are you?"

in the night

awakened
from a deep dream
that is a confusion
playing its dishevelment
as though a conversation
of insensible things
shared
between rational beings

my eyes open
staring at the darkness

startled

I call
where are you
but the silence is a hollow
swallowing sound and equilibrium
in a single gloating

I find that I am panting
and the feeling
of the heart
within my chest
is the gallop
of a panicked steed

I must rise
find the light switch

I need to feel the floor
unmoving
beneath my feet
as I stagger to the kitchen sink
to find a glass of water

to find a calming
that might last me through
until dawn

sough leaves and heartbeat moments (stolen)

But there is only the oak tree rustling in the wind

I
listen in the night
when you are gone
away

keep imagining
the car wheels
turning

the sound of gravel
crushed
beneath tyres

and I think that I can hear
the purring
of the engine

coming home

but no
you have hardly gone

the long hours
stretch
before me

and the sound
I can hear
is only the oak tree
rustling

as the wind
ruffles through
the sough leaves

I turn away

toss and roll

the bed
beneath me
has hardened

there is no comfort
to be had
from lying still
and wondering

about you
and the road

about the place
you are
and where you've been

the night to come
and the long hours
still
before me

the oak tree
sighs

the wind
is her accomplice

and every breath
she sounds
is another moment
taken

I will lose one more
the same
with every heartbeat
(at least)
until you get home

Title: **A Kiss for the Worthy**
ISBN: 978-1-925963-04-5 (pbk)
ISBN: 978-1-925963-05-2 (e-bk)

mmm-hmmm (this day)

I CELEBRATE myself, and sing myself

and here I am
the morning come

I rise again
I rise

the sun serves
to illuminate
this world of mine

I rise to kiss
the light

ray
by ray
and beam
by shining beam

I sing
to myself
a satisfaction
for the knowledge
that I *am*

for the *being*
that is me

I laugh
a little dance
as though a stream
a rill
across the smoothing stones
of the woolshed creek

phwee
phwee-phwee
phwee phwee

I whistle to myself
oh
how I love the day

and how
I love
this day

phwee
phwee-phwee
phwee
phwee

mmm-hmmm

see then sing (then rise)

And what I assume you shall assume

I
will sing songs
as though
the heavens sang

open up
my voice
with great
conviction

and I
will sing
for you

croon
my love of
being
beneath
a southern sky

let you hear
my heart

its rhythm
beating
beating

beating

and you will see
what I see
through the tenor
of my tones
assume
what I assume
is right
within the song

it is
of a dry
and blue
wide heaven
that I sing

of constellations
that populate the night

the southern cross
and
the pointer

so sing with me

come
sing with me

let us
be
our voices

and rise

note
by note

above ourselves

beyond

in the midst I cannot think

For every atom belonging to me as good belongs to you

it is
difficult

to think

in the presence
of my own
self

there are times
when I . . .

the very *fact*
of me
becomes
overwhelming

it is the awareness
of being

the knowledge that
I

am

my thought
is comprised

compromised

by every atom
belonging to me

establishing *me*
in my own awareness
in such a way that
nothing

no-thing

and
no-*other*-one

is established

what glory
is this

what joy

what knowledge

who
can think
while in the midst

the very midst

of their own
being

is beautiful (this year)

I loafe and invite my soul

I will wander
wool gathering
in my mind

as the wind
blows
stray petals of white blossom
shed by the generosity
of the golden plum
before me

a loaf along

my face
to a breeze
that brings the power
of fragrance

the fresh flowers
of spring

and I
invite my soul
to join me

sing
a sabbatical
pastorale

including
the fleeting flash
of red
and the squeaking pitch
of rosellas
shrilly arguing
in waking branches
of the sentinel oak

what better wool
than this
to gather

what better awareness
of spring

could there be anything
better
than to *be*
residing
as one
with my soul

the pink
of the peach
is beautiful
this year

Rescue and Redemption

Title: **Rescue and Redemption**
ISBN: 978-0-9751442-9-9 (pbk)
ISBN: 978-1-925963-03-8 (e-bk)

blather

S'io credesse che mia risposta fosse

If I but thought that my response were made

how could I explain
the truth

my truth

so at odds
with his

sometimes
I feel that I
have lived
too long

too
over long

and the words that form
inside my mouth
are ancient
understandings

the times
have changed
and he
has no ears to hear
such sentiments

and so
I mumble
crumbs
of now stale
cake

dry

difficult
to swallow

until
one of us
must turn away

heart filled
with
mis-
understandings

and we wonder
each of us
alone

what
just happened

he believed
my answer
was so much cant
and
so much blather

I believed
with all my heart
that I wished
to be heard

by him

this once

this
last time
that I
can love him

yesterday (never does)

A persona che mai tornasse al mondo

To one perhaps returning to the world

here's to you
my darling

here's
to you

ever since you left
I have found myself
secluded

cotton-woolled

alone
in a darkness
of my own making

I could do
this

or
I could do that

I could
so many
many
things

other than hide away
as I do
in the darkness left
behind you

for a time
I hoped
that you would come back
to help me fill the world
around me

for a time
I thought
that yesterday
lived on

it never does
and nor
did you return
into this world
of I
alone

here's to you

here is
to darkness

here
is me

the flickering (stilled)

Questa fiamma staria senza piu scosse

This tongue of flame would cease to flicker

always
the flame has danced

I
have danced along
inside

the flickering
is a sign
of life
a-glow

to dance within
is a sign that reads
alive

that reads
living

it is the soul
I speak of
here

the soul
that is the spark

it is the soul of me
and the way I know
I am one
with all

with
everything

but the flame
is staring
now

the flame
is still

frozen
in mid flicker

no more
tremoring

no more dance

and I
am staring

and still

I
hold no
flicker

and find the flame
gone cold

a sculpture
in colours
correct

the shape
perfect
in contour

but frozen
as my soul
is frozen

empty
of all warmth

I glance around

all else is blue
and white
and shadow

(at least) I will know

I will say no more
of reasons

madness
is its own
cause

and ever
there is more to find
more
to draw upon

to deploy

and if I did
well
what now
can I tell
to explain it

I grant myself
one respite

only one
that must
suffice

and that is
that I drew away
before completing
execution

each of us
carries
sorry wounds

each of us
not really
healing

each
building moats
and walls
and stately barricades

to weep
behind

and hide
within

to nurse our losses
and begrudgements

my room is small
now

enough
for me

no more
the expansive
the welcoming
the hearty

you must knock
three times

you must rap
a score

you must call my name
aloud
to the heavens
and
at my entryway

I shall not
come

expect no
response

but know that
at some point
I will hear

should you approach
eventually
I
will know

Source Materials

If you would like to find some information about Gaston Bachelard, whose work I drew upon for *A Love Poetry Trilogy*, the Wikipedia links are here:

Amy Lowell: *https://en.wikipedia.org/wiki/Amy_Lowell*
Walt Whitman: *https://en.wikipedia.org/wiki/Walt_Whitman*
T. S. Eliot: *https://en.wikipedia.org/wiki/T._S._Eliot*

I have accessed the source poems from the following locations:

The Reader (Madonna of the Evening Flowers):
https://www.thereader.org.uk/featured-poem-madonna-of-the-evening-flowers-by-amy-lowell/

The Walt Whitman Archive (Leaves of Grass):
https://whitmanarchive.org/published/LG/1891/poems/27

The Poetry Foundation (The Love Song of J. Alfred Prufrock):
https://www.poetryfoundation.org/poetrymagazine/poems/44212/the-love-song-of-j-alfred-prufrock

I commend these wonderful organisations.

FP

Author Information

About Frank Prem

Frank Prem has been a storytelling poet since his teenage years. He has been a psychiatric nurse through all of his professional career, which now exceeds forty years.

He has been published in magazines, online zines and anthologies in Australia, and in a number of other countries, and has both performed and recorded his work as spoken word.

He lives with his wife in the beautiful township of Beechworth in North East Victoria, Australia.

Connect with Frank

As the author, I hope you enjoyed *Pebbles to Poems*. I think that mine is a unique style of writing that can appeal well beyond a *'pure poetry'* readership.

If you enjoyed it, I'd like to ask you to do two small things for me.

First, take a moment to find your favourite online retail store by using the universal link for *Pebbles to Poems* **https://books2read.com/Pebbles-to-poems**, and leave a short review of the book in your preferred store. The book is also listed and may be reviewed on the Goodreads site.

Online reviews provide social proof to readers and are critical to Indie authors such as myself.

The second thing is, please pop over to my author page **www.FrankPrem.com**, and subscribe to receive my occasional Newsletter.

From time to time I'll let you know what is happening with myself and my writing, as well as keeping you informed of any giveaways I may be planning.

You can also find me on Facebook and Twitter.

Other Published Work

Collaborations

Herja, Devastation – Frank Prem, Cage Dunn (2019)

Anthologies

Short Stories of Forest and Fantasy: Fantasy Anthology by OzTales(2019)

Aquarius: Speculative Fiction Inspired by the Zodiac (The Zodiac Series) by Deadset Press (2020)

Stories of Hope Stories of Hope: Bushfire Relief Anthology by Aussie Speculative Fiction (2020)

This Is Lockdown by M. J. Mallon (et al) (2020)

What Readers Say

Small Town Kid

5.0 out of 5 stars

A modern-day minstrel

As a 'New Australian' of eastern European heritage, much of Frenki's life resonates with me, and yet it's the imagery of time and place that makes these poems familiar to all Australians. And perhaps to non-Australians as well. Boyhood and the wonder years. Some things are universal.

Highly recommended

—A. F. (Australia)

5.0 out of 5

Small-Town Kid is a wonderful collection

With so few words Frank is able to paint a picture so vivid you can't help but get lost in the story. Whether he's talking about family, a picnic, a trip to the butcher or even the outside toilet it's difficult not become immersed in the words and imagine yourself right there with him. Cover to cover, this is an excellent read.

—S. T. (Australia)

5.0 out of 5 stars

A poet's walk through his childhood in a small Australian town.

From the dedication poem, 'I Can Hardly Wait to Show You', to 'Circular Square Town', Frank Prem's chronological journey from infancy to the present has a familiar feel to it, almost as if you were taking a walk through your own memory lane to recall the innumerable small, but unforgettable moments that make up a life.

—J. L. (USA)

Devil In The Wind

5.0 out of 5 stars

I live in the US, and though I recall these fires, I never knew the personal stories behind them. Frank Prem instantly grips you by the throat in his step-by-step story of survival.

I was especially taken because he told the story through poetry, which I've never related to this way. It was stark and vivid, the language of a survivor. It's a quick read, but trust me, this book will stay with you.

Bravo!

—K. K. (USA)

5.0 out of 5 stars

Very moving, beautiful, and terrible

—J. S. (South Africa)

5.0 out of 5 stars

Outstanding!

I'm not normally a reader of poetry, but Devil in the Wind captured the essence of 7 February 2009, and the days and weeks afterwards, with eloquence and ease. Beautifully written, the author has given a human voice to those who matter. Highly recommended.

—B. T. (Australia)

The New Asylum

5.0 out of 5 stars

Brilliant succinct memoir. These insightful, thought provoking behind-the-scene stories are woven so seamlessly you'll lose track of time. 'this somebody's boy' is one of many which will hold your heart.

__M.P-B. (Australia)

5.0 out of 5 stars

Words can't do justice to the emotional journey I travelled in (reading this collection). I don't think anything can. My heart bled, my eyes burned. And I will read it again, to remind me.

__C. D. (Australia)

5.0 out of 5 stars

"The eternal asylums of mental health ...another shift in the backwards."

If I had to pick one book over the past year that has truly resonated with me, this would be it. It's a hauntingly beautiful window into the successes and failures of working with the mentally disabled, and the impact on the human psyche.

__K. B. (USA)

Walk Away Silver Heart

5.0 out of 5 stars

Frank Prem has an extraordinary way with words and his poems invoke great passion and emotion in the reader. This latest work is inspired by a poem called Madonna of the Evening Flowers by Amy Lowell. The poet has taken each line of this famous poem and used it to inspire his own poem.
—R C (United States)

5.0 out of 5 stars

As Memorable as My Favorite Music

For me, the entire book felt like such a beautiful way to show the depth of intimacy, appreciation, knowing, and longing at times the man in the poem has for his love.

—M D (United States)

5.0 out of 5 stars

Prem's style is different from Lowell's, more like chains with each link composed of a word or three, yet he captures the tone and language of Lowell's poem with lovely originality. Each response becomes a glimpse, and combined, they encapsulate a graceful reflection on a loving relationship. There's a sense of depth and maturity in the feelings it evokes. A beautiful collection.

—D P (United States)

A Kiss For The Worthy

5.0 out of 5 stars

A Celebration of Life Written in Thoughtful Bursts of Poetic Expression

This author, much like Whitman, celebrates his philosophy of life and humanity written in thoughtful bursts of poetic expression.

—C M C (United States)

5.0 out of 5 stars

A fascinating poetry collection!

A beautiful, empowering poetry collection, by Australian author Frank Prem, takes you on a journey of love, healing, self-discovery, inner strength, and personal transformation. A trip through uplifting feelings that grow from seeds and change into flowers.

Recommending to true poetry-lovers!

—A N I (United States)

5.0 out of 5 stars

With every verse, I found myself reflecting about myself, my life, and the world. Frank Prem is wonderful at evoking emotions and memories, masterfully connecting them with observations about nature, life, and the world. I loved how simplistic yet meaningful each line was, I just loved every poem.

—K

Rescue and Redemption

5.0 out of 5 stars

The passion of love in its many forms explored by one for another.

(Prem's) unique minimalist style gets to the heart of the matter, where the meaning is found between the framework of the words. It's the kind of deep meaning that one feels but may have difficulty expressing verbally. Frank's skill in finding a way to the heart dwells in the realm of the spiritual.

Favorite poems are: "(at least) I will know," "words (not today",) "alive (is what you feel,)" "what (feels real)," "elation (two times)," "as much as is needed," "white face (and rhyme)," "novel advice (my darlings)", and "of rock pools (and responses.)"

—J L (United States)

5.0 out of 5 stars

Refresh your heart and mind

Frank Prem writes poetry which has a flow and intent that is addictive. It makes you laugh, nod in agreement and also has moments of sadness as it reminds us of how fleeting some precious moments can be.

—S C (United States)

5.0 out of 5 stars

This is the third book in the series. The final.
I've enjoyed every word, every breath. Every moment within the life of these stories.
If you enjoy the style, the movement, of these pieces, you're in good company.
The poetry is refreshing, direct, deeply felt.
Enjoy.

—C D (Australia)

Herja, Devastation

5.0 out of 5 stars

How does a reader give this work the credit it deserves? Simply written, powerfully felt. A man with a job, a woman he loves beyond sanity (or is it his only hold on sanity?).

He is her tool, he says, and I feel the depth of that longing to be nothing more than that. Loved it. Can't say that enough.

__C. (Australia)

5.0 out of 5 stars

The cover alone was enough to excite me to look inside. I'm glad I did.

I loved this book. I don't know whether to call it poetry or prose, and I'd never heard of Eddic tales, but if that's your thing, or you want to feel the subtle menace, albeit from a loving hand.

This is a book I will reread and remember for a long, long time.

__C. (Australia)

5.0 out of 5 stars

As a combination of poetry, prose, and wonderfully ominous illustrations, I found Herja, Devastation refreshingly original. The narrative slipped seamlessly between the two forms and the valkyrie/assassin story carried my interest throughout.

Highly recommended!

—G. B. (Australia)

FrankPrem.com